Rehab at the Florida Avenue Grill

Rehab at the Florida Avenue Grill

Veneta Masson

Copyright © 1999 by Veneta Masson
First Edition
Second printing 2006
ISBN-10: 0-9673688-0-4
ISBN-13: 978-0-9673688-0-1

Library of Congress Catalog Card Number 99-90707

Printed in the United States of America by
HBP Charter Inc., Alexandria, Virginia.

Please address all inquiries to:
Sage Femme Press
PO Box 32124
Washington, DC 20007

Cover photograph by James L. Hall

Design by Lisa Carey Design, LLC
Alexandria, Virginia

What the soul does for the body,
the poet does for her people.

epitaph of
Gabriela Mistral

Contents

Fundamentals of Nursing

Just Who

Nurses

A baby's born. Its first faint cry is drowned
in mother's tears both for what is and for
what should have been—a perfect child. Around
them nurses set about their healing chores.

A breast is gone and in its place a gash
across the very heart of womanhood
still bleeds in tiny kills. Unabashed
a nurse keeps vigil, willing loss to good.

A beam collapsed and left him less a man.
He rattles bedrails, pelts the air with curses.
A nurse confronts him eye to eye and hand
to trembling hand.
    I want to ask these nurses

Do you face the dark because you trust in light?
Or is it that you've come to terms with night? ○

The Language of Hearts

Morning Report

Standing at attention
in the damp dawn
of my novitiate
I take down
everything I need to know
about his deteriorating condition—
scheduled labs and consults
the machines and their quirks
the tubes, meds and procedures that
    please God
will keep him alive,
at least through my shift.

But nothing of what I was told
has prepared me for what I find
in the hectic clutter of bedsheets—
        a man
a small man
with rheumy eyes
and sleep-creased cheeks.
I stand watching, drenched in unease.
Wait! He stirs,
slowly at first
then jerks a shaking hand
from some hidden fold.

Bang! You're dead,
he says with a grin
through cracked lips,
trigger finger leveled
straight at my head.
I snap to life at this morning report
and the burden of dread falls away.
Face to face with vitality
still venting itself
from this body of death,
I am struck by the force
I must reckon with. ○

The Language of Hearts

The hearts of the old beat like talking drums
or so I imagine each time I sound
a leathery chest through a stethoscope.

My ears pick up the syllables — animated snaps
and clicks, distant hums, murmurs and sighs
riotous thumps like something falling downstairs.

I've been studying the language of hearts.
Old ones have the most to tell
and tell the most of how they came

to ache, break, leap, sink, melt, turn to stone.
When the old folks ask me what I've heard
I always tell the truth. It's regular

as a clock, I say, or working hard though it skips
a beat or two. But never have I heard
the half of all their hearts contain. ○

Old Arthur

Old Arthur sweeps in just ahead of the rain
tweaks elbows and knees
carelessly squeezes fingers and toes
leaves them bent like stalks in a field
then plants himself at the base of a spine
yawns his way down a leg uninvited,
a poor relation who comes on a whim
and might settle in for the winter.
The old folks wince and shake their heads
pray he'll be gone with a change in the weather. ∘

Snowbound

So we are snowbound
in a snowbound city
where only "essential" employees
reported to work.

Surely we are essential,
or at least I am,
to one or two if not to all

    to Sadie perhaps
    or Sultana or Nellie
    Alma
    Alberta
    or Herman.

Invalids, they are homebound
not just today but all year round.

Who will dress their wounds if not we?
Who will bring them their pills?
Who will hear their frail hearts
    and scarred lungs
    and night fears
    if not we — or me?

But we are snowbound.
On the telephone
we agonize over the fact
that we're frozen in place.

Surely it is essential
to get to them, isn't it?
To one or two if not to all?

    Yet all have survived
    except Herman who died
    quietly
    this morning
    in his chair. ○

The Promise

If you could just lose weight
your blood pressure would go down
your diabetes would clear up
you could get off all those pills you take
your joints wouldn't ache
you could climb the stairs
run after the bus
carry the groceries
pick up the baby
the swelling in your legs would go down
you could reach all the way to your aching feet
you could breathe again

You could find clothes to fit
get out of those slippers and into real shoes
who knows but what your old man would come back
you'd get more respect from your children
a decent job
your son would kick drugs
your daughter wouldn't get pregnant again
you'd live to see your last one grown

Your neighbors wouldn't talk about you
the toilet would flush
the roof wouldn't leak
there'd be food enough at the end of the month
they wouldn't cut off your check
jack up the rent
you'd hit the number
go off for two weeks in Aruba

Jesus would save the world from sin
those who mourn would be comforted
the poor would enter the Kingdom of God
your hunger would be filled. ○

Rite of Spring

What is it about Spring—
all these women coming in
dressed like flowers,
perfumed in lilac and rose?
It's a clinic after all
not a nursery.

But seldom is anything
what it appears.
A radiant smile masks uncertainty
and questions lie hidden
in symptoms like pain
and unexplained changes in rhythm.

It's been a year or two
or forever — and nothing.
And here's a husband buzzing about
seeding the nights with diligence
and the days with expectation.
Now, another negative test.

How to conceive this failure?
If woman's life is not for this
to what end all her artifice?
And if it is...

Consider these lilies
　　taking thought
　　taking thought
　　taking thought for tomorrow. ○

Passages

Tragic!
The day shift said that afternoon when I came on duty.
She's 35 and dying of uterine cancer.
Yes, he's still there, sitting beside her—
       he seems to want us to leave them alone.
Imagine how he must feel, after all
       a gynecologist
       watching his wife
       die on account of his impotence.
At least she's too far gone to feel the pain.

Tragic! I echoed, looked down at my feet
       stuffed my notes and my hands into pockets.
At 20, I was a novice still
       and ill at ease
       with the celebration
       of mysteries.
Reluctantly, I began my rounds, knowing that door
       at the end of the hall
       was one I had to open.

The moment came. I knocked lightly and entered.
First I saw her, or rather the barely perceptible
        rise and fall
        of the caul
        of luminous sheets.
Then I saw him, eyes fixed on the IV drip
        as if on an hour glass
        watching the last few
        grains of sand run through.

I want to talk with you, he said as I worked
        then followed me out when I left the room.
Where in God's name have you been? he exploded.
For hours no one has opened that door!
        And then in a small
        and stubbed out voice
How do you know if she's dead or alive?
There's nobody with her but me.
        I'm sorry, I said, and stood there.

He was 40, a physician, and powerless
        to stop this traitor womb
        from giving birth to death.
I wanted to say, but hadn't the words
        What can I do?
        You are the healer.
I didn't know then the things I know now about how it is
        that nurses heal
        and healers fail

        and face the face of loss again and again.
Many times I've wanted to find him, touch him
        as I couldn't do then
        let his eyes sink into mine
        hear him down to the roots of his words
        practice now familiar rites of nurturance.
And yet, if he asked, I would have to confess
        I am 40, a healer, and still don't know
        a remedy for despair. ○

Exposure

Here I am
watching the blood
flow over the palm
of my open hand.

Warm, dark, laden with secrets
about to be told
it fills the glass tube
that rests in the palm
of my waiting hand.

I am watching you
watch me
watch the blood
flow from your vein
in a needle-fine spray
into the red-top tube.

Our faces reveal nothing
but under duress
reduced to a film of serum and cells
the blood will confess.
As yet nothing has been exposed
except the blood. ○

Lower Midline Surgical Scar

I see so many
so many scarred women
who cannot tell me
why they were cut
what was taken or
how it changed them.

They say
There was a tumor...
I bled...
The pain...
I was pregnant...
I'm not really sure...

I touch these scars
one by one
day after day,
describe them all
in the same four words
for the record.

Is there more to say
or feel
about a minor breach
of integrity
in a complex body
of evidence?

Well healed, I might write—
the clinician's
seal of approval.
But how do I know
what lies below
the surface—

still palpable relief?
benign regret?
anxiety?
or a hot and throbbing memory
that rankles wordlessly
within? ○

Guilt

The ER phones with
  a sick little girl
  under your care for a year
and now
critical
with surgery
standing by.

What can I do?
My daughter is dying!
  the mother had said
  two months ago
  and again and again
  but tests showed
  nothing.

Just look at her!
the mother had said.
  I did
  and saw the light
  in those mischievous eyes
  dimming out
  drowned in maternal anxiety.

Questions, regrets
hang in the air
and guilt
    like a vise with jaws
    that crush compassion
frets at objectivity
diminishes all it touches.

They've got no case.
I've done no harm
I think
as I voice concern
    and every growing
    part of me is reduced
    to a charred dark cinder. ○

Boutique

I'm a nurse, I replied
wondering why the salesclerk asked
and wishing I were something exotic
 a poet in exile
 an entrepreneur
 a spy undercover
or something more —
more what?
something more.

I can believe it, the salesclerk said
in response to my words
 (not my wishes)
Why?
Because of the earrings
 I chose to try on?
my face, gait, style?
some mark to which I'm oblivious?

I could never do that, she said
   but I'm glad you can.
Can what? Can what that she can't
   or won't?
Usually it's bedpans and blood
   they fix on.
For me that's life, nothing more
   nothing less.

Why did you ask? I ask.
Her answer is only a smile
   and the price of the earrings.
And why was I tempted
to lie
   or tell some other truth?
I try on some glittery ones
check for effect in the mirror
   decide not to buy. ∘

Deliverance

To swaddle a struggling toddler
facing a painful procedure
we use a papoose board.
Its four strips of canvas
fastened with Velcro
fix arms and legs and head
to a mummy-shaped slab.

Little José, at thirteen months
too strong to be held,
lies on the board
one arm extended.
Terrified, he throws his head
side to side,
screams.

Above him his mother
hovers, an engine
of instinct.
In one fluid move
she lets down her full breast
massive, warm
the color of earth.

It covers his face
is all he can see
all he has to hold on to.
His open mouth roots around wildly
fills with the nipple
latches on
sucks. ○

The Attentive Nurse

after the portrait by Chardin, c. 1738

In her hand she holds an egg not a lamp
though the artist brings her out of the kitchen
shadows with light from his palette.
She's dressed modestly in quiet shades.
A square-bibbed apron covers her skirt
and a head kerchief her willful curls
but lace at the face and throat
shows us she is no kitchen maid.
Patiently she lifts the shell from the
top of the egg she's cooked herself
places it next to the bread and medicinal
wine on the linen tablecloth.
Imagine her cajoling the elderly invalid
with deference and tempered wit
mindful of his frailties, attending to his
bilious whims and cravings.

Not so many years ago in the glare of
a modern hospital room, I stood by a bed
with an egg in my hand, ordered by
an implacable patient to take it
back to the kitchen and inform the chef
he'd cooked it too long. Boiling inside
I wanted to ask if he thought the dietary staff
should be bothered with minutiae
and what did he take me for— a maid?
Keeping my wits, I went off with the egg
came back with another and placed it
next to the toast and bagged Lipton's tea
on the plastic breakfast tray.
Imagine me nursing the ill-tempered invalid
mindfully, and with grace in the face
of injured professional pride. ○

The Screamer in Room 4

This toddler glares at me
from her mother's lap.
Her eyes are sharp as tacks
black as coals.
She greets me with a scream
will not let me touch her
or cajole a momentary lull
in the hostilities.
Mother does not intervene
makes no apologetic coos
no irritated reprimand
no sound at all.

Are we playing house?

Let's see, mommy is high
and daddy went bye-bye
before you were born
and mommy's new friend
has a violent streak
brother is hyper
big sister won't speak
grandma is angry
but what can she do?
So who does that make you
little screamer?
Who does that make you? ○

The Gift

She is desperate, depressed
a job on the line
relationships strained
remaining friends say,
Get help!

I give her what I as a nurse
have to give — medicinal time
a finely tuned ear
other parts of myself
I have honed into instruments.

One day she arrives with a gift.
A mirror framed in sterling,
it fits in my palm.
In it I see myself clearly,
too clearly.

Quickly slipping it back
in its soft black pouch,
I say thanks, and reflect —
this is the same gift
all my patients give me. ∘

Fundamentals of Nursing

Admission

Her eyes would blur
so she couldn't see
to fill the syringes.
Often as not
she'd skip the dose
and damn the diabetes.

She'd get groggy
so she'd lose her balance
    and fall—
bound to break a hip one day
land in the hospital
die of complications.

The most complicated things
are simple
in the beginning.

I offer a house call
to check her sugar
and fill the syringes
a week at a time

I offer to enter
once every week
an uncharted world
not my own.

Enter, do for, exit
    Simple!
Enter, look around, listen
    do for, exit

Enter, wonder
Enter, ask

Enter deeper
Enter ○

A Sixty-Year-Old Black Female
   With a History

Yes, Lord!
With that huge record collection
she was a shrink's delight —
    crazy jazz, delusional blues
    all the famous labels.
For a while she was positively addicted,
kept her stash of dancing shoes
    in the closet
but when love died
there was only the hard stuff
to turn to at night.
Not to mention the ruptured ectopic
that left a scar across her belly —
    never did heal.
She burned, baby, to where she had
to give up her job as a nanny —
    said she just couldn't stomach it.

Ended up with smoking lungs —
    took cigarettes for the cough.
On account of no resistance
she came down with a string
of chronic boyfriends, rings
on every finger, every doorbell —
    even a thing
    for the drugstore delivery man.
She still suffers degenerate joints
whenever she can get out to one
but the shoes are her biggest regret —
    feet so swollen
    and she never could
    dance barefoot. ○

Home Remedies for the Blues

Front door locked
doesn't answer the knock

    but I have a key

She stands at the window
looking out, looking down

    I go to the kitchen
    make coffee

Sullen, she nonetheless
lets herself be lured to the table
lifts her mug
shifts in her seat

There are three ways to do it
she says at last

    Do what? I ask

*Jump out the window
poison or... you know...*

    What do I know?

This! she says
and flicks one scarred wrist
with a whisk
of the other hand

    Keep talking, I say

She does ○

Side Effects

For a mental case
her symptoms aren't impressive.
Over the years she's taken her meds,
gone off now and then,
moved in and out of Saint E's.

Inevitably there are side effects.
What bothers her most
is how her jaw and face muscles work
as if she were forced to chew and chew
on something she cannot swallow.

Well, what the hell—
it's the price you pay
for staying alive.

Sporting red sweats that match her nails
and an upswept do from the beauty school
she flashes a wide, lascivious grin

> *Child, look at me!*
> *I'm a big woman*
> *with style!*

There's no such thing as a side effect—
only a palette of givens.
She took what she got.
Now here she stands—
proud artist become her own canvas. ○

Care of the Sole

The ulcer on her sole
ate away at her.
She couldn't feel it
see it or reach it
but her fear of it
was palpable.

> *Am I gonna lose my leg? she'd ask*
> *I'm gonna lose it, I know.*

It was a litany we said
for the care of her sole.

> I: It's a bit smaller (or bigger) today
> She: *I'm gonna lose it*

> The color is pinker (or grayer)
> *I'm gonna lose it*

> The foot is less (or more) swollen
> *I'm gonna lose it*

> You have to stay off it
> *Lord, Lord*

> And you've got to keep your sugar down
> *Lord, O my Lord*

This went on for months, years
until her fear proved justified
though ironically
it was the other she lost
to sudden, unchecked infection.

One foot in the grave, the other decayed,
she tried suicide before deciding
that any sort of a life would suffice
and she'd do what she could
to care for her ravaged sole.

    One day at a time
    One day at a time

    Lord, she crooned
    Lord, O my Lord

    Ain't nobody
    knows my name ○

Rehab at the Florida Avenue Grill

Edging down the crowded aisles
and into a booth
on one bum leg
    (the other lost
    two months ago to sugar)
is no picnic
but here she is
a.m.a.
drizzling maple syrup on hotcakes
as an old boyfriend sidles up
starts talking sweet
and asks her for her number.

Ain't got no phone, baby
    she lies, smiling
    shrugging him off
    reluctantly.

She knows too much sugar
poured on all at once
can be risky for someone like her—
    hungry
    and out of control. ○

    a.m.a.—against medical advice

The Next Leg

She jettisons her wooden leg
like so much ballast
then careens across the room
in her wheelchair
with the pitch and roll
of a ship sailing into a storm.
She is foundering.

Something's wrong, baby!
Tell me what's wrong!
I can't talk right
I'm dropping things
and I'm sick to death
of being cooped up!

She's right about something
being wrong, but what?
I am at sea,
with that queasy feeling
that precedes rational knowing.
As for her, she knows
what she knows.

Pills?
    No!
Hospital?
    No!
Doctor?
    No!
Check back tomorrow?
    Yeah, I spose so

But I'm anchored fast
unable to cast off and go.
I stand behind her
kneading her shoulders
taking her bearings
steadying us for the next leg
of the journey. ○

Occupational Therapy

I heard it first
from the pharmacist.
The pharmacist! who delivered
her pills once a month
or whenever I phoned him.
I heard it first
first thing this morning
calling him up
for some routine thing
not news — not this news
he'd had from the sister
who'd stopped by her place
and found her
splayed out on the floor
"just cooling off" —
the sensible sister
who later thought
to phone the drugstore
to cancel all refills.

And the nurse?

Ah well, I see.
I'm not family
and not strictly business,
more like a pair
of helping hands
and a vigilant voice
at the end of the line
without a face or name.
I sit staring down
at my idled hands
and the loose ends
of another loss
unraveled in my lap.
Quick! Spool them up.
Foolish to squander sentiment
on grief, when one day you'll find
you're of a mind to take up
the threads of memory
and fabricate something practical

    a skein of remembrance
    a counterpane
    a poem ○

Just Who

Maggie Jones

Just
who do you think you are, Maggie Jones
following me home from work
insinuating yourself into my evening
shading my thoughts?

Just
who do you think you are
lying flat as a pancake in the middle of your bed
your world ranged around you in brown paper bags?

(Rather like a dead Pharaoh in his tomb, I'd say
buried with all his treasure)

So you fell one day and had to be taken
    to the hospital.
You didn't break any bones, after all.
You came home in a taxi
climbed the steep flight of stairs to your room
took to your bed and stayed there.
That was three years ago, Maggie
three years with only one thing to look forward to—
    livin'.

I'm here by the hand of the Lord, you always say
    when I come
though the hand of the Lord didn't smite the rat
    that bit your foot
    that cold winter day last year
    as it foraged in your sheets for bread and jelly.
I guess it'll be all right
    you said in your genteel way
    looking up at me with soft doe eyes as I dressed
    the wound that brought us together.

Why don't you go to a home? we ask, shocked
    to see the condition you're in
    (the church ladies, the social worker
    your niece, your nephew and I).
Because I still have my right mind
    you say simply.

    A nursing home is no place
    for someone who still has their mind.

But it's not safe here, we say
    (the church ladies, the social worker
    your niece, your nephew and I).
Don't you know they shoot drugs
    and people in this neighborhood?
I've never been bothered
    you say, matter-of-factly.

What about fire? we say
    (the church ladies, the social worker
    your niece, your nephew and I).
There was a fire once, and the fireman carried me out.
I own my home and I own my grave plot
    and I plan to go from one to the other
    when the Lord calls me
    you say quietly, clutching a packet
    of long, white envelopes.

But now your gas is cut off
    until you come up with $700.
You're lucky it's not freezing and there's an electric
    coffee maker we can use to heat water to wash you.
I guess the money will come from somewhere
    you say, looking at me steadily.

And Meals on Wheels has cut you off because it's a bad
    neighborhood to begin with and then
    the front door fell off its hinges
    onto the Meals on Wheels delivery lady.
I guess there's enough food in the United States
    to feed me
    you say, looking at me knowingly.

And
they've taken away your homemaker because they say
    you need more care
    than the agency can give.
I guess things will work out
    you say, looking at me trustingly.

How can you lie there and say, serenely, you guess
    things will work out?

    Your room is cold
    your sheets are soaked with urine
    your skin is bleeding from bedsores
    you don't know where your next meal is coming from
    you're a poor old lady
    hidden away
    in a falling-down house
    in a no-good neighborhood.
    And you have expectations?

You told your niece not to worry about you
    the nurse was coming.
Hey, Maggie Jones, don't wait for me, don't count on me.
    I'll bathe you
    dress your wounds
    treat your minor ailments
    even do your laundry and bring you food
    once in a while.
But save you?
God alone—the hand of the Lord—can save you.

I see you now in my mind's eye and wonder
    as I sit
    after dinner
    in my warm house
    on a safe street
    in a good neighborhood
Just
who do you think you are, Maggie Jones? ○

The Ladies' Marching Society

The Ladies' Marching Society, she calls them
and when she calls, they come
for she, you see, is the dying one
(though it is never said, she won't permit it).
From efficiencies and one-bedrooms
past rows of shut doors
they advance toward the sound of her moaning.
Calm and forbearing, they come bearing gifts of
    finely chopped chicken
    fresh pasta from Dino's
    beef consommé
    smooth vichyssoise
    even medicinal brandy.

Stiff and tight lipped, they retreat
having learned that
    the chicken meat is white and dry
        instead of dark and juicy
    the pasta is cold
        and underseasoned
    the consommé is liquid
        she wants jellied
    the lumpy soup's an insult
        to her palate
    the brandy is Hennessy Special
        instead of Triple X
        Ghastly!
        She broke her glass in shock
        when she sipped it.

Ladies of the Marching Society
who live in staid retirement
are awed by the power of one of their frailest own.
They wait at attention, offer small talk
then lean down to ask her
    What would you...?
    How can we...?
    Mercy! Surely you don't...?
    A Delmonico steak and champagne?
    For breakfast?
    Darling, please don't shout, just tell us
    What would you...?
    How can we...?

Members of the Marching Society
    accept abuse patiently
    stand by loyally
    make distressed telephone calls nightly
    are wan and white knuckled ordinarily
      but especially when on duty. o

On Hearing the News
of a Patient's Death

Morning light glances off the chrome
    of a stripped down car in the alley
slices through window panes
    along the edges of drawn shades
opens fire on sheets pulled up
    to shield the eyes of sleepers.

This summer sun won't light your eyes.
Not even the cries of the baby reach you.
It's too late, for you went early
just as we thought you might
    but not like this
    manacled to a bed
    in the maternity ward
    of D.C. General Hospital.

Hearing the news, I call up your face
a wide-open face with a slow shy smile
as if the shock of life had somehow dazed you.
You took each day
    each man
    each child
    each welfare check
    each jail cell
    as it came.

It just wasn't in you to ask why or why not
to look ahead or behind.
Since when does someone like you get to choose?
Since when do poor ignorant women take charge
    of their lives?

The world for you was
    your mother's house, teeming with kin
    the street
    the welfare office
    hospital and
    jail.
A heroin high was the only place you ever had
    to call your own
and a fix was the only way you knew
    to get there.
The judge decided to keep you in jail
those last few months of your pregnancy—
the best he could do for your unborn child.
Why bring another addict into the world?

Oh, it isn't that you never tried to kick.
You'd come to us in pain
    with abscesses from dirty needles.
You'd come when the drug supply dried up.
You'd come when there was no money to buy.
You'd come when you felt too tired to sell.

I can do it alone, you said
    I can kick.
Just give me a few Valiums.
A little help is all I need.

I suppose we'll never know just how you died.
It was after the baby was born
after they'd taken you back to the ward.
Some people said they heard calls for help.
When they found you, you were hanging
    over the side of the bed
    dangling by the foot
    they'd shackled to the bedframe.

Your family set up a wail that went on for days
        alleged foul play
        hinted at revenge.
There was gunfire at the wake, they say
and eight motherless children destined for
        your mother's house
        the street
        the welfare office
        hospital and
        jail.

The last light you saw in the blank night
        of your life
was your newborn girl.
Is that why you named her Star? ○

The Arithmetic of Nurses

S-s-s, S-s-s, S-s-s
Bennie Smith is trying to speak.
I am counting out cookies
from a faded blue tin.

S-s-s, S-s-s, S-s-s
Twelve!
Are twelve cookies enough to hold
a sick old man for thirty-six hours?
Twelve cookies and one can of juice?
Twelve cookies wrapped in a towel
tucked under a pillow where roaches
ply a brisk trade in crumbs?

Six!
He blurts it out
face lit up by the restless flicker
of the television screen.
No, twelve, I muse.
Unless someone comes
that's all he'll have
till I get back again.

S-s-s-six thousand!
He strains under the weight of the words.
Clearly he has something important to say
but I am caught up with my own calculations—

The number of minutes
it will take a rivulet of urine
to reach the screaming bedsores
on his back

The number of degrees
his temperature will rise
as infection sets in

The number of days
it will take him
to let me call the ambulance

The number of times
I must walk the long hall
to this dim little room
the width of a bed.

His stiff body straddles the low bed
like a piece of plywood on a sawhorse.
Push down on the feet, up comes the head.
I tilt my ear toward his mouth
to catch the stutterings.

S-s-s-six thousand nurses...
on strike today...
Meh- Meh- Meh- Minnesota!

Half his face breaks into a grin
for if there's one thing Bennie understands
it's the arithmetic of nurses
and old, abandoned men. ∘

How Are You Today,
Miss Nellie?

My ass is sinking into a hole.
It's black and deep
with puny little afternoon stars
that float behind my eyes
and noise as white as snow.
That's what comes of never getting
all the way up in the morning.

That old man holding up
his face to be kissed
told me I was dead.
Just like you he came
too early. All the same
I'll want a box that doesn't
leak when it rains. ○

Litany of Dolores

Ay, que bonita viene.

> Chimes from the church across the street
> mark the hours of my visits, chime ten
> or two or four as I climb the dark stairs
> pull open the knobless door of the room
> where you lie like a broken doll
> waiting for me as if for the fresh-faced child
> who may forget to come, having so many
> other, more precious possessions.

Que Dios le bendiga, Dios le pague.

> God will repay the small mercies I offer —
> hot coffee, an ear to receive your confessions
> aspirin, bandages, pair after pair of shoes
> you can't wear because of the fire
> that is melting your joints.
> And yet you, too, are a giver of gifts —
> creams and perfumes by Estée Lauder
> strings of beads from the toe of a stocking
> a black paper fan you got from your sister
> Revlon's Finest Professional Emery Boards.

Viera como me duele.

> You left your country, your mother's house
> to help your sister raise her infant son
> and the shock of her death ignited a fire
> deep in your bones. Marcos, too, is consumed
> with bitterness. Looking at you, he rails
> at the God who took his wife.
> You could have had her! he cries
> Why did you not take her instead?

Todo lo malo que hace se paga.

> The fire inside flashes up in your eyes
> and your chin juts out when you speak
> of the evils that Marcos has done
> in the time since Lydia died.
> He won't let you turn on the heat or light
> took away the TV set, brings you nothing
> but rice at the end of the day, though he
> fixes frijoles and meat for himself. Worst of
> all he's set the child against you, encouraged
> him in petty cruelties—laughed when he marked
> up your body with crayons. Yes, God will
> repay the evils of Marcos. All he's done will
> be repaid.

Perdone que le moleste.

Forgive me, you say, for talking like this
and pardon me for bothering you, but hand me
my stick with the nail on the end,
a threaded needle to mend this sweater.
I think there is a clean towel in that bag,
some medicine for the pain, perhaps
a spray of cologne behind my ears
and pardon me, pardon me, pardon me.

Quiero caminar. ¡Voy a caminar!

There were days when you spoke of walking again
and days in summer when hope hung sweet
and ripe as the mangoes of home. You stood
gripping the rails of your walker, inching through
the doors toward the stairs that led
to the kitchen. One day I will be happy, you said
but by the time you reached the third step
your strength was gone. No more, you said, no more.

Quiero que sea comigo cuando yo muero.

I have closed your eyes, washed away
the burning heat of your fever, laid you out
in the lavender gown, hung the necklace
I brought from Copán around your neck.
The child and I sit side by side
drinking the sodas I sent him to buy,
paging through the album you asked me to hide.
There are pictures of women and children and seasons.
We look at the book and talk of your life
and stop when we reach the blank pages.

Phone Call to Edward

I'm in the emergency room
with tubes all in me
and oxen on.
Now listen good
and do what I say.
Feed the cats
and don't forget
the shy one who stays
in the back of the yard.
Put the money away
in the place you know.
Don't tell anyone
where I am and
don't go out
on the street at night.

Take the check
that's under the doily
and carry it down
to pay the electric.
Don't lock yourself out
like you did last time.
You can boil the chicken
and heat up the greens.
If the plumber calls back
you give him what for
and don't come down here
to see me, the fare's
too high. I'll let you
know when I'm coming home.
I'm hanging up now
cause I'm short of wind
and the nurse is here
to take the phone.
Water my plants
but not too much.
Just do it like
you seen me do.

You know mens.
They've got no sense. ∘

Ruination

Still fierce after fifty
years of fighting
    now for
        now against him,
she threw off the news
of his death
like just another
blow out of nowhere.

Killed by procedures,
she was to say
though no one
at the hospital
told her anything.

After the bleak little funeral
attended mostly by
stacked metal chairs
she came back
to the mildew-stained
rooms they had shared
got rid of the wig

the stiff black dress
    the never-worn pumps
    that hobbled her feet
and installed herself on the sofa
in front of the mound of clothes.

Then she commenced
to rip
one by one
the shirts
    the pants
        every garment he'd owned,
to tear them in strips
and bag them
for burning.

We all have to die sometime,
the man down the hall had mumbled
then greedily asked
what she planned to do
with the clothes.

Rip
    tear
        bag
            burn

Fingers gnarled, unbendable,
fists long years past clenching
but strong
    strong
       strong enough
for this task come to hand.

I reckon it will take three weeks,
she said
without troubling herself
to look up.

    How long it took
    was nobody's business
    but hers.

Rip
    tear
        bag
            burn

            return
        return
    return
return ∘

Gangster Cool

When his girlfriends called
they'd ask for Gangster Cool.
That was his street name.
He had this gang of little boys
thirteen, fourteen
so whenever he threatened
his sister he'd say,
I don't have to hurt you myself
I can get someone your own
age to do it. He's violent
when he doesn't get his way.
One time he lay there watching me
get his son dressed
for day care. Something I did
must have set him off
cause all of a sudden he's on
his feet, his hands fisted up
his lip shooting out
in that way he had. Called me
a big fat dumb old bitch
unfit to raise a child.
Oh yeah, I said
Well I raised you!

There was only one person
he used to look up to
when he was a child.
His grand-daddy took him
to church every week
whupped him, kept him
in line. But when
grand-daddy got to be
sixty, the boy figured out
there was nothing more
he could do.
Grand-daddy
got it figured out, too
but still he'd post bail
whenever the boy got
locked-up — and never once
a word of thanks.
The boy was too busy
calling his friends, shoutin'
I'm free, I'm free!

That picture you saw
when you came in the door—
the one of a man—
the unfinished one—
it's one of his. I hung it
there to cover the hole he
punched in the wall when he
found out his brother had taken
his jacket. He locked me into
my room that night cause he
thought I'd try to call the police.
It's true I wanted him
out of here but it was no use.
What the police used to say
comes down to this, Ma'am,
he's your son. There's nothing
to do with no one killed.
You'll have to handle it
best you can. And you wonder
why my pressure stays up...

It did no good to change
the locks. He'd break
the door down, stomp in and say
in his bully voice,
I'm stayin' here, see
and I want some respect.
He didn't care about me.
Oh he loved me, sure
cause I'm his mother
but the only one he
cared for was himself.
Lately he seemed to be
spending more time with
his art—he learned to paint
in jail. People were
starting to buy the sad
faces, dark and fierce
like his except they had
tears. But drugs
earned him more and drugs
are what killed him.
Last night they found him
dead on the street. It was
nobody's fault. I know it had
to've been a fight over drugs
or money. He was never one
to back down.

Funny how just that
afternoon we talked
on the phone. I was
going to court on account
of him and the boy was
talking as sweet as you please.
Now Ma, he said
do what you have to but
don't tell the judge
I was beating on you
or something like that.
If it makes you feel
better I swear I won't
come back to the house.
A few hours later
the phone rang again
and someone was yellin'
Gangster Cool's been
shot in the head!

Gangster Fool! was all
I could say. That's what
I called him. I couldn't
cry. It was like all my
tears ended up on the faces
he painted. That picture
he gave you —
the one with two faces
one old and one young.
I want to see it again.
In all the confusion
I can't remember —
I want to know — which one
of the two is crying. ∘

Ticket to Christmas

That day, that Christmas Eve last year
I went to work as usual, but full of expectation.
I went to the clinic expecting Christmas
to happen to me. I thought I knew what it would be—
most probably a patient and a poignant interruption
in the flow of everyday. There might be merriment
or tears. There would be touch. I'd touch
and let myself be touched by Christmas.

All morning patients came and went.
Some laughed. One wept.
I touched them and was touched in turn.
But none of them was Christmas.
By afternoon, I knew there was something more
I needed to do. I'd go to the market
across the street, buy cookies and punch
and set them out in the waiting room
like a child making ready for Santa.

There wasn't much time, patients were waiting.
I threw on my coat and ran out the door
just in time to catch a green light.
But a voice called out from the P Street side
of the liquor store. Christmas had been there
waiting for me. Startled, I stopped
missed the light, stepped backwards
up, onto the curb. There wasn't much time.
Patients were waiting. I deeply resented
the interruption even though I knew who it was.

Christmas was black, fifty or so, wearing
an Oriole's baseball cap. He swayed a little
but didn't reek and started to speak as if
he had something to say I needed to hear.
I'm homeless, he said, and then he told
how long ago he'd prayed to God to show him
how it was to live on the streets, but just today
he'd been telling God he'd had enough.
Where will you spend the night? I asked.
In the shelter at Second and D, he said.

He wanted to give me a present. I wanted
to make the light. I knew he was Christmas
but I was uneasy and wanted to be on my way.
Wait! he said and started to empty his
pockets into my hands: a red and green bag
with a pair of white socks, a lottery ticket
he made me scratch while he halted the search
(we didn't win), folded papers, a tattered
social security card and so on down to the lint
in the seams until at last he found it.

"Admit One" is what it said. A ticket to
the Christmas gala the city puts on for
down and outs. *Take it*, he said. *I've seen
it all — the stars, the food, the fancy decorations.
But don't go dressed like you are right now.
Go home and change into something a homeless
person might wear so you can feel just what
it's like. You get my meaning, don't you, Miss?*

I waited for the hustle. It never came.
He never asked for money or a date.
I put the ticket into my pocket and left him
when the light turned green. As I made my way
to the grocery store I heard his voice
behind me once more. *Miss!* he called
*Remember that's my ticket. Remember
that ticket's my Christmas gift to you.* ○

Epiphany at Maggie's

One thing was clear as I came down the stairs—
she held the low ground between me and the door
by dint of nothing more than her hunkered frame
and low-pitched warning growl.
Perhaps she knew that patch of wooden slats
was all she'd get out of life, except abuse
and the scraps of food that fell from
old Maggie's bed. Time after time
I'd schemed to win the mutt over—
conversed in dulcet tones, brought food.
She knew too much to trust the likes
of those who used this crumbling house
(by no one's leave) to shoot up, crash
or slip a practiced hand in Maggie's
coin purse while she slept.
I tried to make the point that I was different—
here to help, deserving of safe passage.
I talked, I smiled, I opened my hands.
She bared her teeth, her tail went down.
So I got tough and rattled the banister.
She glared and the whites of her eyes turned red.
Holding my breath, I eased down one step.
She stiffened, snarled, but did not move.

As if caught in a searchlight
we froze in our poses, considering
how this stand-off would end.
Two minutes passed.
Then out of the blue, a dark figure loomed,
threw open the door and glanced up at me.
You comin' out? Well go on then, he said
and yanked the bitch by the neck
to the back of the stairwell.
I made my escape, but relieved as I was
it still seemed unfair
that the match was thrown
and I was free
and casual epiphanies like these
are what our fates are hung on. ○

Cheers for Bobby

One infection
Two infections
Three infections
Four
Floxin
Doxy
Penicillin
More.

His name is Bobby
He looks real good
He's known all over
This neighborhood.

Hey, Bobby!
Ooh, Bobby!
Sweet Bobby!
Yes!
How many ladies?
Anybody's guess.

Sophisticated Bobby
Everybody knows
Sophisticated Bobby
Everybody knows.

Five infections
Six infections
Seven infections
Eight
Clap and Chlamydia
Alternate

With itchy rashes
Open sores
But Bobby's twenty
And out to score —

Get a shot!
Take a pill!
That's what they're
There for.

Hot shot Bobby
Everybody knows
Hot shot Bobby
Everybody knows.

Nine infections
Ten infections
Eleven infections
Twelve
Bobby's not
Countin'
What the
Hell
Is he thinking of?
Is he thinking?
Hey Bobby
What are you thinking of?

Listen to your mama
Listen to your friends
Can't you see
How this will end?

Drip dick Bobby
Everybody knows
Drip dick Bobby
Everybody knows.

Five short years
Less fifty pounds
Fevers
Curtain
Comin'
Down.

Yes, life's a stage
You've played a role
That's hard to fathom
Hard to own

And even you don't
Know what's there
Behind that deathless
Mask you wear.

Sick sick Bobby
Everybody knows
Sick sick Bobby
Everybody knows.

Ring around the rosary
Pockets full of poetry
Ashes, ashes
We all fall down. ◦

Another Case of
Chronic Pelvic Pain

Like the others, she is not from here
and when she came she left
all of what matters behind —
four children, a village
a father (not well), the lingering
scent of her man (who had fled)
Sunday walks in the plaza after mass
on days when the soldiers were gone
on days when no bodies were found.

The journey from home was perilous —
sometimes on foot, or crowded
into the back of a truck, over hills
through dense forests, arroyos
dark rivers, toward menacing lights,
the eyes of hostile cities.

The trip cost her more than
she wanted to pay—
all the crumpled bills
from the earthenware jar
in the wall of the house,
the silver bracelets and earrings
passed down from her mother.
Her body they took along the way
again and again as if for a debt
that can never be paid.
What drove her on was a woman's
fixed and singular faith that
she is the giver of life
the mother of God.

By bus from the border
by phone from the station
by foot to the room of the friend
of a cousin who knew of a place
and jobs cleaning offices at night
where no questions were asked
and dollars were paid
unless you missed work
or were caught by the migra—
all this distance she came
numb to the pain in her feet and back
and the ache in her lower heart.

She spent her days trying to sleep.
Nights she roamed large empty halls
as wide as the streets
that gave onto the plaza
pushing a cart full of cleaning supplies
bagging the trash, sweeping the floors
washing away the stains of another
day in the upper world.
Paydays she sent her money home
by the man at Urgente Express.
Sunday she sometimes walked
down the street at the edge
of the park, watching
with shaded eyes among the men
for one she might know.

Months passed this way
and with each one she wept
the tears of blood that women weep
and felt the ache in her belly
grow stronger until at last
there was no relief,
come new moon or full,
and no poultice, tea or prayer
that helped her bear
what she must bear.

She sits in the clinic—
"a 32-year-old Hispanic female
complaining of chronic pelvic pain."

The results of all the tests
are negative, they say.
That means there's nothing we can find
to blame for all the pain.
There is a cause, of course—
perhaps a scar deep inside.
Surgery might tell us more—or not,
but then there's the matter of money.

I see, she says simply.
*Well, if you can't find
anything wrong—and you know
there is no money...*

There are some pills
you could take, they say,
for the pain, when it
bothers you most.

You are kind, she says
and stands up to go,
like the others,
from here to her job,
her room, and perhaps twice a year
to a telephone that spans the miles
of dense forest, dark river
to the house of a friend
of an aunt of her father
to ask if the children
are well and in school
on days when the soldiers are gone
on days when no bodies are found.

I will send for them
one day soon, she says.
For now there is only the ache in her belly,
come new moon or full,
and no poultice, pill or prayer
to help her bear
what she must bear.

What drives her on is a woman's
fixed and singular faith that
she is the giver of life
the mother of God. ○

Acknowledgments

My thanks to the editors of the following publications in which some of these poems first appeared: *Capital Nursing:* "Exposure"; *Geriatric Nursing:* "Ruination"; *Hungry as we are* (Washington Writers' Publishing House, 1995): "Deliverance"; *The Journal of Christian Healing:* "The Language of Hearts"; *Journal of Christian Nursing:* "Maggie Jones"; *Mediphors:* "Old Arthur"; *Nursing and Health Care Perspectives:* "The Attentive Nurse," "Boutique," "The Gift"; *Nursing Outlook:* "On Hearing the News of a Patient's Death"; *Nursing Spectrum:* "Nurses," "Passages"; *Potomac Review:* "Home Remedies for the Blues," "Rehab at the Florida Avenue Grill."

"Snowbound" appears with permission from *Nursing Spectrum*, Washington, D.C./Baltimore Metro Edition. Copyright © February 18, 1991.

The following poems are copyrighted by the *Journal of the American Medical Association* and appear with permission:
"The Promise" 1994:272(19) 1482e
"The Screamer in Room 4" 1996:275(7) 574f
"Morning Report" 1997:277(6) 444f

The poems in the last section (with the exception of "Ruination") first appeared in *Just Who*, published in 1993 by Crossroad Health Ministry, Inc., Copyright ©Veneta Masson.

Thanks be...

to The Thanks Be To Grandmother Winifred Foundation
for a grant that has helped turn this
collection of poems into a book

to the D.C. Commission on the Arts and Humanities,
and the National Endowment for the Arts, for partial
funding of this project through an artist's grant

to Doris Bloch, friend and colleague who doesn't much
like poetry but likes these poems, for her encourage-
ment and proofreader's eye

to Lisa Carey, for the grace of her design and the atten-
tion she has lavished on this small testament

to Jim Hall, physician and colleague of many years, for
the cover photograph, "Miss Mattie and the
L Street Crew"

and, always, to my husband, Frank, for his love and
support through all the years these poems encompass

About the Author

I was a nurse before I was a poet.
For thirty-five years, I practiced
as a registered nurse in communi-
ties, homes and hospitals both
in the United States and abroad.
In the late 1970s, I helped
to found a small, inner-city clinic in Washington, D.C.
called Community Medical Care.

The impetus for the poems in this collection came
during the seventeen years I was part of CMC. Many
of them started as journal entries written in satisfaction,
sorrow, confusion or frustration at the end of a day.
Months or years later, crafted into poems, a number of
them found their way into the clinic's annual reports,
professional or literary periodicals and, finally, into the
hands of other caregivers and readers of poetry.

I still live in Washington, still frequent the neighborhood
of the old clinic (now relocated to another part of the
city and absorbed into a large network of non-profit
clinics), my patients' homes (some gone, others renovat-
ed), my church (down the alley from the boarded up
Howard Theater) and the Florida Avenue Grill, a land-
mark in this city that, besides being a world capital, is a
vibrant and diverse hometown. I continue to explore
healing art as a nurse, poet and essayist.